UNITED STATES
AIR FORCE

BY JOHN HAMILTON

VISIT US AT
WWW.ABDOPUBLISHING.COM

Published by ABDO Publishing Company, 8000 West 78th Street, Suite 310, Edina, MN 55439. Copyright ©2012 by Abdo Consulting Group, Inc. International copyrights reserved in all countries. No part of this book may be reproduced in any form without written permission from the publisher. A&D Xtreme™ is a trademark and logo of ABDO Publishing Company.

Printed in the United States of America, North Mankato, Minnesota.
052011
092011

Editor: Sue Hamilton
Graphic Design: Sue Hamilton
Cover Design: John Hamilton
Cover Photo: U.S. Air Force
Interior Photos: Corbis-pg 24; Library of Congress-pgs 7 (inset of Civil War balloon) & 8 (inset of Harry S. Truman); Lockheed-Martin-pgs 28 & 29; U.S. Air Force-pgs 1-23, 25-27, 30-32.

Library of Congress Cataloging-in-Publication Data

Hamilton, John.
   United States Air Force / John Hamilton.
      p. cm. -- (United States armed forces)
   Includes index.
   ISBN 978-1-61783-068-6
   1. United States. Air Force--Juvenile literature. I. Title.
   UG633.H357 2012
   358.00973--dc22

                                    2011013149

CONTENTS

The Air Force uses fighter jets to support ground troops and battle enemy aircraft. It uses unmanned drones for search-and-destroy missions. The Air Force even controls satellites in space.

THE UNITED STATES AIR FORCE

The United States has the most powerful and modern air-fighting force in the world. The United States Air Force can strike an enemy thousands of miles away using missiles and long-range bombers.

AIR FORCE HISTORY

An Eberhart SE-5E
used in World War I.

On December 17, 1903, Orville and Wilbur Wright flew
the first heavier-than-air powered aircraft at Kitty Hawk,
North Carolina.

The Civil War balloon *Intrepid* is inflated in May 1862.

During the Civil War (1861-1865), Union forces used hot air balloons to spy on Confederate troops. When airplanes were first invented, the U.S. Army had little use for them. But during World War I (1914-1918), airplanes became useful and deadly. They were used to spy on the enemy and drop bombs on people and buildings. Aerial duels between planes were called dogfights.

Air power played a major part in World War II (1939-1945), including the dropping of two atomic bombs on Japan. Since then, the U.S. Air Force has played a critical role in most American conflicts, including those in Korea, Vietnam, Yugoslavia, Afghanistan, and Iraq.

The August 1945 atomic bomb blast on Hiroshima, Japan.

On July 26, 1947, President Harry S. Truman signed the National Security Act of 1947. It made the United States Air Force an independent part of America's armed forces.

An F-15E Strike Eagle deploys flares during a mission over Afghanistan.

Air Force recruits on an assault course during basic training.

AIR FORCE TRAINING

Air Force recruits must be between 17 and 27 years old to apply. Basic training is challenging. Recruits become physically fit and learn to use weapons. After training, recruits can go on to become pilots, flight engineers, aerial gunners, airplane mechanics, or many other jobs offered by the Air Force.

AIR FORCE PILOTS

Air Force pilots are highly trained commissioned officers. They must be physically and mentally fit. They must also complete a bachelor's degree program at select colleges. Many choose the U.S. Air Force Academy, near Colorado Springs, Colorado.

An F-16 Fighting Falcon pilot in the skies over Iraq.

XTREME FACT After college and officer training, cadets attend a year-long flight training program. A lucky few will also receive advanced training, learning to fly specialized aircraft like the F-16 Fighting Falcon.

F-16 FIGHTING FALCON

Air Force fighter jets are small, fast, and highly maneuverable. F-16 Fighting Falcons can reach speeds of 1,500 miles per hour (2,414 kph). Many pilots think these planes are the best fighter jets in the world. They can attack other aircraft and ground targets, even in bad weather.

F-22 RAPTOR

F-22 Raptors are fast, highly maneuverable fighters that use stealth technology, making them almost invisible to enemy radar. Designed mainly to fight other aircraft, Raptors can also attack ground targets. Although costly, Raptors are unmatched by any other fighter jets in the world today.

An F-22 Raptor makes a max climb seconds after takeoff.

A formation of F-22 Raptors in a combat training exercise.

B-52 BOMBER

XTREME FACT

From wingtip to wingtip, B-52s measure 185 feet (56 m). They can carry up to 70,000 pounds (31,751 kg) of explosives, including nuclear weapons.

Long-range bombers are designed to carry heavy loads of bombs long distances at great heights. B-52 Stratofortresses were first used in the 1950s. They can fly for thousands of miles. Through continuous upgrades, especially in electronics, the B-52 remains an Air Force workhorse.

B-1 LANCER

Air Force B-1 Lancers are long-range bombers that can fly faster than the speed of sound. They have variable-sweep wings that are pulled back for high-speed flight. Originally designed to carry nuclear weapons during the Cold War, Lancers today carry conventional bombs and missiles.

Two Lancers release chaff and flares while on a training mission.

B-2 SPIRIT

B-2 Spirits are long-range bombers that use stealth technology to evade detection. Their specially coated black skin and "flying wing" design make them almost invisible to enemy radar.

B-2 Spirit bombers have a total program cost of about $2.1 billion per aircraft. There are currently 20 B-2 Spirits flown by the Air Force.

B-2 Spirits can carry many types of bombs and missiles, including nuclear weapons. They have been used in the wars in Iraq and Afghanistan.

MINUTEMAN MISSILES

The interior of a
Minuteman missile silo.

The Air Force maintains an arsenal of about 450 LGM-30 Minuteman III intercontinental ballistic missiles (ICMB). They are meant to keep enemies from using nuclear weapons against the United States. Minuteman missiles are launched from underground silos, and can hit targets on the other side of the world. A single Minuteman warhead can destroy an entire city.

A Minuteman III missile is test launched from Vandenberg Air Force Base in California.

PREDATOR DRONES

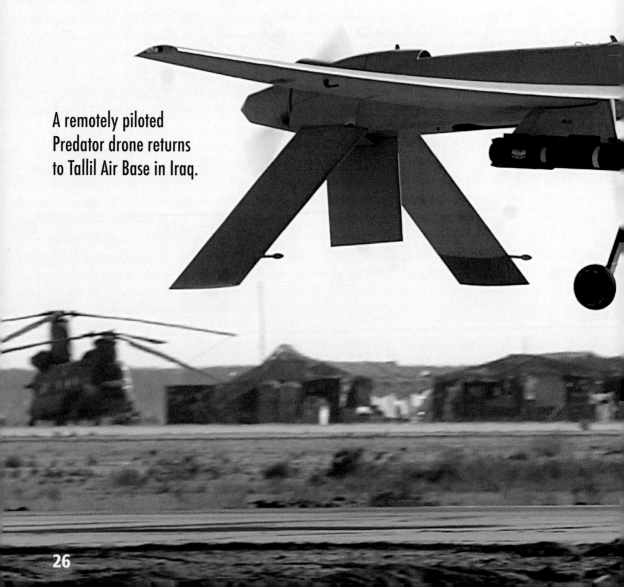

A remotely piloted Predator drone returns to Tallil Air Base in Iraq.

Predator drones are a type of unmanned aerial vehicle (UAV). They are robot planes, flown by Air Force pilots in ground control stations many miles away. Equipped with cameras and sensors, and armed with Hellfire missiles, Predators can fly over targets for many hours before returning to base. Predators have been used extensively in the U.S.-led wars in Iraq and Afghanistan.

THE FUTURE

The U.S. Air Force will continue responding quickly and forcefully to future threats. It will rely on skilled pilots and ground crews, plus advanced technology, to defeat enemy forces anywhere in the world, or even in space.

The F-35 Lightning II is the Air Force's cutting-edge fighter of the future. It is a single-engine, multirole aircraft with stealth capability.

GLOSSARY

BALLISTIC MISSILE

A ballistic missile is an intercontinental, or long-range, missile that is guided only during its ascent into space toward a target. When the missile re-enters Earth's atmosphere, its flight path is determined by physical laws such as gravity. It cannot change its path in mid-flight. It is much like throwing a ball at a very distant target with great precision.

BOMBER

A bomber is an aircraft that has a primary mission of dropping explosives, in the form of bombs or guided missiles, onto enemy ground targets. Bombers are usually large, relatively slow aircraft.

CHAFF

Pieces of foil or clusters of fine metal wires ejected into the air by military planes to create a false target. An enemy's radar mistakes the metal chaff for the target, and anti-aircraft missiles explode in the chaff instead of striking the plane.

COLD WAR

The Cold War was a time of political, economic, and cultural tension between the United States and its allies and the Soviet Union and other Communist nations. It lasted from about 1947, just after the end of World War II, until the early 1990s, when the Soviet Union collapsed and Communism was no longer a major threat to the United States.

FIGHTER

A fighter is an aircraft that is relatively small, fast, and highly maneuverable. It is designed mainly to attack other aircraft, but some fighters can also attack targets on the ground.

MULTIROLE

A fighter aircraft that can perform several types of missions is called a multirole aircraft. These missions include reconnaissance of enemy positions, attacking other aircraft, and attacking targets on the ground.

STEALTH

Aircraft equipped with stealth technology are virtually invisible to enemy radar, infrared, or other detection methods. Stealth technology includes such features as radar-absorbing materials and coatings, streamlined fuselages and wings, plus recessed engines that mask hot exhaust.

INDEX